HOUSE *of* LEARNING

HOUSE *of* LEARNING

Getting More from Your Temple Experience

M. RICHARD WALKER
KATHLEEN H. WALKER

ᛦ®

DESERET
BOOK

SALT LAKE CITY, UTAH

Library of Congress Cataloging-in-Publication Data

Walker, Richard, 1937–
    House of learning : getting more from your temple experience / Richard and Kathleen Walker.
        p. cm.
    Includes bibliographical references and index.
    ISBN 978-1-60641-101-8 (hardbound : alk. paper)
    1. Mormon temples. 2. Temple work (Mormon Church) 3. Temple endowments (Mormon Church) I. Walker, Kathleen, 1939– II. Title.
    BX8643.T4W35 2010
    264'.093—dc22   2010011131

Printed in the United States of America
Worldcolor, Fairfield, PA

10 9 8 7 6 5 4 3 2 1

To the thousands of temple workers
in the Salt Lake Temple who labored with us,
and whose lives of dedication and devotion
were an inspiration to us.

We will always remember you
and be grateful for your example
of lovingkindness.

CONTENTS

INTRODUCTION

Our lives together began on January 31, 2004. We had both lost our spouses some years previously and had come together with a bit of resistance and some trepidation. Forty years of prior marriage, family, career, Church experience, and unique circumstances had brought to each of us a fulfilling and rich life. And so when our circumstances changed and we found ourselves single, we were a bit baffled as to what our future would be. But the Lord saw fit to move us forward, and we were introduced to a new life that brought us together.

We spent the first eighteen months redefining that life, accommodating change, getting to know each other, blending ten children and forty grandchildren. We were assembling a new future. We were so different, and yet so alike.

Richard: My father died just three days before my first birthday. My mother, thirty years old, was left with four young children. On that dark day in June, everything in the life of my family changed. I grew up without a father and with a mother who worked day in and day out to keep our little family together. I missed having a dad, but I came to idolize my mother. And it was my mother who first instilled in me the idea that the temple was a special place.

When we were children we had a Saturday routine. We would get up, laboriously clean the house, and get ready for Sunday. When our chores were completed, we were anxious to get to our play activities. Our mother, on the other hand, would go into the bedroom, pull out a little suitcase, and take it to the ironing board, where she would meticulously press some white clothing. She would then leave the house and go to the temple. We found this so puzzling and hard to understand. We knew she was exhausted from her week of work and her responsibilities at home. We wondered what could possibly have motivated her to go to the temple when she could be home taking a nap or doing something for herself. This became a point of curiosity to me and I determined that someday I would find out why . . . and I did!

Kathleen: When I was sixteen I had occasion to participate in a wedding that was held in a beautiful Protestant church in downtown Salt Lake City. It had all the elements of a storybook event—the preacher in his robes, red carpet down the aisle, rose petals, ring bearer, organ music, and all the rest. I loved it! I felt just like I had stepped into the middle of a romance novel. I was so caught up in the enchantment of it that I began to feel sorry for myself. "I will sacrifice such grandeur," I thought, "because I will be married in the temple. Woe is me!"

It was just a few weeks later that the Los Angeles Temple was dedicated. Because my father had an assignment associated with that event, we made a family trip of it. It was the first time I had ever been in a temple, and I shall never forget the feelings that washed over me when I entered that holy edifice. I stood at the foot of the beautiful sweeping staircase that graces its foyer, and it looked to me like it was coming straight from heaven. All my romantic notions of a wedding returned as I envisioned myself gliding down that staircase, enveloped in love and beauty. But even as I stood there, I knew what

I was feeling was more than just romance. It was a feeling of being drawn to heaven, and I was quite overcome with deep gratitude and resolve that someday I would be married in such a place. I think it was then that the temple began to find a place in my heart.

∞

From those early experiences in our youth, there was born in each of us a deep feeling about the temple. We knew it was special. We knew it was good, and we knew that someday we wanted to be a part of it. And so when we came together, the temple was already an important part of our lives. We didn't know then, however, that it would at some point consume our lives.

After eighteen months of marriage we began to talk about how we could render full-time service in the Church. It was about this time that the unexpected call came for us to serve as president and matron of the Salt Lake Temple.

∞

Richard: I had been serving as an ordinance worker for three years and so I was somewhat familiar with the procedures and responsibilities that came with such a calling. However, I soon came to realize how very little I knew.

Kathleen: I was a little concerned about the calling. I thought that the only thing a sister did in the temple was stand around in white, looking lovely and pointing out directions. I soon came to realize that "ignorance is bliss."

∞

With great feelings of inadequacy, we began our service as the president and matron of the Salt Lake Temple on November 1, 2005. It was as if we had stepped onto a bullet train moving at high speed. We worked as we had never worked before. We had challenges we had never had before. We had demanding hours and consuming responsibilities, as never before. But we also had the most beautiful, inspiring, and edifying experience of our lives. We worked alongside the most dedicated and spiritually committed people that could be found anyplace in the Church. We learned and laughed and loved. And we felt our lives change on a daily basis.

Almost immediately we both came to understand that the Lord governs His holy house and there is so much to learn under His tutelage. The great key is to gain understanding of the spiritual meaning of the symbolic teachings of the temple. Consider the Savior's parables—the process of understanding them comes with continuous study, pondering, prayer, and deep searching. Only then can we grasp the spiritual meaning of the parables. So it is with the temple. Understanding its spiritual meaning begins with a personal desire and preparation of our lives to receive through the Spirit.

We also came to understand that the temple is all about our Heavenly Father and His Son, Jesus Christ. It is truly the Lord's spiritual university on earth. It teaches us the plan of happiness and opens the gateway to eternal exaltation, which cannot be obtained without the covenants and blessings of the temple.

When we were called to this assignment, we were told that this would be the crowning experience of our Church service—never before and never again would we do anything that would compare with it. So true! When you spend most of your time in the house of the Lord, your life changes.

We found it fascinating that people go to the temple in all stages of preparation and understanding (or lack thereof). Some go because they feel an obligation to go; some go seeking peace from the trials and burdens of life; some go out of curiosity; and some go just out of habit. Many go because they are motivated by the spirit of Elijah to perform the work for their kindred dead. And many go to learn and seek understanding of the Lord's eternal plan for them and their families.

It is wonderful to go to the temple for any reason, but just putting a warm body in a seat in the temple is not enough. We have observed patrons sleeping, checking their watches, even text messaging. Perhaps just a quiet respite from the world is enough for them. Perhaps that satisfies their current need, but there is so much more available to anyone who has a desire to seek it and a willingness to search and unlock the spiritual meaning of the temple ordinances.

We have talked with many patrons who express a desire to understand more but do not know how to open the learning process of finding personal meaning in the eternal principles taught in all areas of the temple. It was with this in mind that we created this book. In it, we will suggest to the reader ways in which the temple can become a personal spiritual university. We have personally found excitement and new knowledge as we have begun to unlock the spiritual understanding of the ordinances and how they apply in our lives. Even today, we continue our quest of learning as we attend many different temples of the Church. We hope the same for you.

Part 1

PREPARING
FOR TEMPLE WORSHIP

Chapter 1

IT BEGINS IN
THE HEART

For where your treasure is,

there will your heart be also.

MATTHEW 6:21

s we began our three-year journey in the temple, we quickly recognized that our ability to understand the spiritual meaning of its symbolic teachings was directly connected to the spiritual condition of our hearts. Normally we were required to arise at what felt like an unearthly hour. On those many mornings, as part of our wake-up process, and in an effort to appear alive and alert, we would often look at each other and ask, "Is your heart ready for this day?" The question sometimes made us groan, but we understood that our hearts had to be pure and prepared in order to understand the things of God taught in the temple. As we continually tried to condition our hearts, our ability to understand the spiritual meaning of the ordinances was greatly enlarged. For this reason we ask you to bring *your* heart as you take this journey with us.

There is an internationally recognized traveling exhibit entitled "Body Worlds, The Story of the Heart." This exhibit centers on the development of the human body and is so powerful that one would have a hard time not accepting the fact that the human body could only have been created by a divine, intelligent, and loving Heavenly Father. The day we visited, we spent several hours viewing the various stages of human development. Over and over again we were profoundly impressed and awed by the magnificence of the divine creation of the human body. We reflected on the teachings of Elder Russell M. Nelson: "Think of the genesis of a human body. . . . Twenty-three chromosomes from each parent unite in one new cell. . . . Approximately 22 days after these cells unite, a tiny heart begins to beat" ("Faith in Jesus Christ," 25).

One of the video presentations in the Body Worlds display explains that the first organ to function and give life to the body is the heart, and the last organ to stop functioning and end life is the heart. A nearby display board made the following statement: "Given all we know about the brain and the heart, emotions and love are still perceived to originate in the heart." This is not new news to those who understand the Lord's teachings concerning the heart.

The Lord created in each human being a heart, which symbolically becomes the center for the power of God's love to grow and develop inside the human body. Through proper exercise of the gift of moral agency, this power of love will expand our capacity to become like God.

The Savior taught of the childlike qualities essential for each of us to develop spiritually. What is it about a child that is such a key to spiritual growth? Clearly it is the purity of a child's heart, untainted and uncluttered by the world. A child sees and understands things with a pureness that often fades as people age and allow the world to influence their lives.

∞

Kathleen: One day a young family came to the Salt Lake Temple to be sealed. A mother, father, and two little boys had prepared themselves for this beautiful and blessed day in their lives. After the sealing of the parents was completed, the two little boys were taken upstairs. As they exited the elevator and turned the corner toward the sealing room, the four-year-old stopped. With eyes full of love and wonder, he looked up and down and all around, and then in hushed tones said, "Where is Jesus? I know He is here!" Tears flowed from those around him as all felt the purity of this young boy's heart.

❧

The Savior's challenge to each of us is: "Except ye be converted, and become as little children, ye shall not enter into the kingdom of heaven. Whosoever therefore shall humble himself as this little child, the same is greatest in the kingdom of heaven" (Matthew 18:3–4).

This challenge requires constant attention and vigilance on our part to prevent the world from contaminating our hearts. In other words, every choice we make influences the spirituality of our hearts. The language we use, the clothes we wear, the places we go, the things we read and watch, are all taken into our minds and directly influence our hearts. It's as the adage related to computers states: *Garbage In—Garbage Out.* The flip side of this statement might be: *Goodness In—Goodness Out.* The spiritual development of our hearts is controlled by the daily decisions we make. The world would oppose our spiritual development.

The prophet Nephi warned us of the plan of the

adversary, which would impede the process of spiritually developing our hearts: "Wherefore, men are free according to the flesh; and all things are given them which are expedient unto man. And they are free to choose liberty and eternal life, through the great Mediator of all men, or to choose captivity and death, according to the captivity and power of the devil; for he seeketh that all men might be miserable like unto himself" (2 Nephi 2:27).

Those who determine to make the choices that will enable them to follow the Savior on a daily basis will find that their hearts change, that they no longer have the desire to follow the world. They find joy in service to the Lord and to their fellow men, even though they live in the midst of a tumultuous world.

∞

Richard: Some time ago a couple came to the temple in response to a letter inviting them to serve. As we talked with them, the wife was very reticent. She felt incapable of memorization and worried whether or not she fit the mold of a temple worker. But when the question was asked, "Are you willing to accept a call to serve in the temple?" she responded, "That decision was made the moment we got your letter." Although fears and

Those who determine to make the choices

that will enable them to follow the Savior

on a daily basis will find that their

hearts change, that they no longer have

the desire to follow the world.

doubts were in their minds, their hearts were pure, and their decision to serve was the natural response of hearts purified through years of commitment and service to others.

∞

When the Pharisee asked the Savior: "Which is the great commandment in the law? Jesus said unto him, Thou shalt love the Lord thy God with all thy heart, and with all thy soul, and with all thy mind. This is the first and great commandment" (Matthew 22:36–38). Because the heart is the origin of physical life, it is also the origin of love. It must be pure in order to understand and follow the things of God.

When King Benjamin called the Nephites to the temple to give them his last address, he said: "Open your ears that ye may hear, and your hearts that ye may understand, . . . that the mysteries of God may be unfolded to your view" (Mosiah 2:9). Those who go to the temple with hearts prepared will make themselves available to the impressions and personal experiences we all desire, even personal revelation.

The scriptures are replete with teachings that emphasize the importance of the heart in understanding God. In Helaman 3:35, Helaman said of the faithful that they "did wax . . . firmer in the faith of Christ, *unto the filling their souls with joy and consolation, yea, even to the purifying and the sanctification of their hearts, which sanctification cometh because of their yielding their hearts unto God"* (emphasis added).

Nephi taught this of the glory of the Millennium: "Because of the righteousness of his people, Satan has no power . . . for he hath no power over the hearts of the people, for they dwell in righteousness (1 Nephi 22:26).

And Alma admonished his people: "I wish from the inmost part of my heart . . . that ye would . . . be led by the Holy Spirit, becoming humble, meek, submissive, patient, full of love and all long-suffering, . . . having the love of God always in your hearts" (Alma 13:27–29).

∽

Kathleen: Another couple who came to the temple to be interviewed for a call to serve there told of how the experiences of their lives had convinced them that they needed to make a sacrifice of service to the Lord to somehow repay Him for all their blessings. They had volunteered and served two missions, back-to-back, thinking each would be a sacrifice. The wife said: "We wanted to do something really hard for the Lord, but the sacrifice always turned out to be a great blessing. We hope our service in the temple will really be hard and allow us to sacrifice and prove our love to the Lord." It is obvious that their search for the "really hard sacrifice" will instead continue to be a great blessing in their lives because their choices have truly purified their hearts.

At a stake conference we attended, a young man, recently baptized into the Church, shared his testimony and stated: "It is so fun to be a teenager when you make the right choices." The heart truly is the control center of the human body. This is why the Savior said: "For I, the Lord, will judge all men according to their works, *according to the desire of their hearts*" (D&C 137:9; emphasis added).

Today in the world of modern medicine, there is much news about the miraculous advances that enable surgeons to perform open-heart surgery on the human body. Likewise, the Lord can and will perform spiritual heart surgery on us as we go the temple with hearts prepared to receive. This process was described by Alma the Younger when he recounted the experience of his father, Alma, responding to the teachings of Abinadi:

"And according to his faith there was a mighty change wrought in his heart . . . and a mighty change was also wrought in their hearts, and they humbled themselves and put their trust in the true and living God. . . . And now behold, I ask of you, my brethren of the church, have ye spiritually been born of God? Have ye received his image in your countenances? Have ye experienced this *mighty change in your hearts?* . . . Can ye look up to God at that day with a pure heart and clean hands?" (Alma 5:12–14, 19; emphasis added).

∞

Richard: One day a rather mature couple came to the temple to be married. I was asked to perform their sealing. As I entered the room, I noticed immediately that they were not your usual couple. The bride was in her late forties, which set her apart from most of the youthful brides. She was a rather ordinary-looking woman from South America who had lived a hard life, including abusive relationships, a child born out of wedlock, and years of dissipation outside the Church. Then the Spirit began to touch her heart. She was introduced to the Church, and her heart was ready to receive. She came to the United States and met a fine man whose heart was full of love for the Lord and love for her. Together they committed their lives to one another and began to prepare to go to the temple to be married.

That day, as they entered the sealing room, the Spirit radiated from them. Their happiness and gratitude for the blessings of eternity spilled over and it was as if everyone in the room felt the deep love and the refined purity that rested in their hearts. As I began to perform their sealing, it was as though they were transformed before our eyes, and we saw this remarkably beautiful, worthy, and pure couple kneeling at the altar, their hearts filled with love for their Heavenly Father, for the temple, and for each other. Their hearts had been changed! Their hearts were pure and they were clean before God. On that day, in that sealing room, I believe they experienced complete joy.

∽

Elder Gerald Lund has said that "the condition of our hearts directly affects our sensitivity to spiritual things. Let us make it a part of our everyday striving to open our hearts to the Spirit. Since we are the guardians of our hearts, we can choose to do so" ("Opening Our Hearts," 34).

When we go to the temple, there are many things we do physically to prepare ourselves. Such things as getting a babysitter, putting dinner in the oven, cleaning our desk, and changing our clothes are all part of preparing physically to step out of our everyday world for a time. We should then begin to think about the temple, to try to lay the world aside in our hearts as well. We should examine our lives and ask ourselves whether there are any conditions there that would interfere with the Spirit. Are we truly worthy? Have we been dishonest in our dealings? Have we offended one of our family members or neighbors? Is there anything we could amend that would better allow the Spirit to teach us as we worship? Are we trying to purify our hearts?

Every two years we sit with our priesthood leaders and review the questions of temple worthiness. One of the most far-reaching questions requires us to evaluate our own worthiness to enter the temple. This is a question we should ask ourselves on an ongoing basis.

The heart is the very center of life, both physically and spiritually. In order for our hearts to remain physically and spiritually healthy, we need to make daily choices that will form habits of righteousness, enabling our hearts to progress in purity.

What am I doing to purify my
heart and prepare myself to
understand the spiritual things of
God as taught in the temple?

Chapter 2

THE POWER OF LOVE

Eye hath not seen, nor ear heard,

neither have entered into the heart of man,

the things which God hath prepared

for them that love him.

1 CORINTHIANS 2:9

Years ago, a movie was released titled *Love Is a Many-Splendored Thing*. When we were young we would sing the title song from that movie. Back then, it was just a beautiful song with nice words and a lilting melody. But when we began to serve in the temple, the words of that song came back to us and we began to understand, in a new way, that love *truly is* a many-splendored thing. The splendor of the love we feel in the temple is magnified because it is the love of God.

⬭

Kathleen: One day we greeted a couple who were sitting in the celestial room waiting for their marriage to be performed. They did not fit the stereotype of most couples, who are young, innocent, and full of the future. The groom was 98 years of age and the bride was 87. They had met in the retirement center where they both lived. As we greeted them, he said, with tears in his eyes, "Isn't she beautiful! I'm so excited. And I was so afraid someone else would get her before I did. This is just the beginning for us!" They glowed with the love of two mature hearts, taking on a youthful countenance.

⬭

One of the great messages of the temple concerns the power of love. It is the greatest power in all the world. "God is love; and he that dwelleth in love dwelleth in God, and God in him" (1 John 4:16). If we truly believe that God is love, then we also will understand that the temple, as a house of God, is a house of love.

In our three years of service in the Salt Lake Temple, we learned in profound ways that 3300 people can work in

If we truly believe that God is love,

then we also will understand

that the temple, as a house of God,

is a house of love.

harmony and be unified through the power of love. That spirit of love transcends all other concerns in the temple. The power of love as experienced among family members, with neighbors and friends, and in so many areas of our lives culminates in the house of the Lord. There a loving Heavenly Father teaches us through the Holy Spirit how to follow a pattern of life that will lead each of us, with our families, back to live with Him.

In addition, through sacred, eternally binding ordinances He lovingly allows us to participate in joining generations of families together. Through this process we are blessed to share in accomplishing the mission of the Savior, which He defined as follows: "For behold, this is my work and my glory—to bring to pass the immortality and eternal life of man" (Moses 1:39). We have been taught in "The Family: A Proclamation to the World" that "the family is central to the Creator's plan for the eternal destiny of His children" (paragraph 1). It is through the temple, the house of God, His house of love, that the power of God's love provides for us the binding ordinances that link the human family to God.

LOVE OF FAMILY

The power of love is what binds a family together, parent to child, child to child, and child to parent. As Elder Dallin H. Oaks has taught: "The eternal truth that our Heavenly Father loves all his children is an immensely powerful idea. It is especially powerful when children can visualize it through the love and sacrifice of their earthly parents. Love is the most powerful force in the world" ("Powerful Ideas," 25).

∞

Richard: Having lost my father at an early age, my mother became my anchor, my idol, and my inspiration. As I grew I watched her work and struggle and toil to care for her four small children. I noticed how she always put us first and often went without so we had what we needed. I knelt with her every night and listened to her pray. One night, as a young man, I had cause to get out of bed and go upstairs. As I passed her bedroom door I heard her pleading with Heavenly Father to bless and protect me. She said how much she loved me and that I was a choice and special boy. That moment was ingrained indelibly into my heart and soul. I can still remember several times in my teens being in bad circumstances and facing difficult choices, and the vision of my mother on her knees would wash over me and I found the strength to walk away. Isn't it remarkable how those simple words and acts of love from a parent can establish firm guideposts in children's lives to enable them to avoid the pitfalls that face them? So it is in the house of the Lord. The words of love from our Heavenly Father that permeate the ordinances of the temple will place guideposts in our lives to enable us to see more clearly as we journey amidst the chaos of the world.

In "The Family: A Proclamation to the World," we are told: "Husband and wife have a solemn responsibility to love and care for each other and for their children. . . . Parents have a sacred duty to rear their children in love and righteousness, . . . to teach them to love and serve one another. . . . Husbands and wives—mothers and fathers—will be held accountable before God for the discharge of these obligations" (paragraph 6).

It is clear that the personality of a child is in great part formed through the power and example of love demonstrated in the family unit. The proclamation on the family is a guide to understanding the love of God for His children, truths about which are taught in the temple.

LOVE OF FRIENDS

"This is my commandment, That ye love one another, as I have loved you. Greater love hath no man than this, that a man lay down his life for his friends" (John 15:12–13).

∞

Richard: About thirty years ago, while serving as a battery commander in the National Guard, I had occasion to fly out to Dugway Proving Grounds in western Utah on a reconnaissance mission. There were three other battery commanders, a pilot (a good friend), and a copilot. We landed on a dirt strip, and after completing our task we reboarded the aircraft. We were told that because of the wind change and the heavy load we would have to take off on a 90-degree angle to the landing strip. On takeoff the copilot discovered that there was a mound of dirt directly in front of us. He attempted to raise the nose of the airplane, which caused the back of the plane to strike the dirt strip, freezing all control of the aircraft except the ability to increase or decrease power. The much more experienced pilot took over. They both had their feet up on the steering mechanism attempting to keep the nose down. They were calling "Mayday, Mayday" over the radio. The pilot said to us, "We can't get the airplane any higher, and I am confident we will crash if we attempt to land. We all have parachutes and although I know that I can survive a jump, I am not sure you can. It is your choice. However, if you choose not to jump, I will stay with you and attempt to land the plane."

We chose not to jump. The airplane did crash upon landing and was damaged beyond repair, but no one was injured. The board of inquiry later concluded that we owed our lives to the pilot who was willing to risk his life in order to save us.

Knowing the possible danger to his own life, the pilot could easily have been motivated by the drive of the natural man for self-preservation. He could have chosen to jump out of the aircraft, knowing he would be safe. But the influence of the power of love in his heart impelled him to face the possibility of injury or death in order to preserve our lives. In that moment of crisis, love became the controlling force, and he chose to try to save our lives—at the risk of his own life. His choice not only preserved my life but has forever magnified my understanding of the power of love.

The second greatest commandment is to love thy neighbor as thyself. The Savior said: "A new commandment I give unto you, That ye love one another; as I have loved you, that ye also love one another. By this shall all men know that ye are my disciples, if ye have love one to another" (John 13:34–35).

There are thousands of people who volunteer their time to serve in the temples across the world. They serve without monetary compensation and give their time in an atmosphere of love for one another. Within the walls of any temple you find a brotherly love that exceeds almost anything found elsewhere in the world. The millions of patrons who attend the temple to worship and serve do so out of love. Every day people come into the temples of the Lord with family file cards in hand to complete the great uniting ordinances for those in their family line. It is not uncommon to find families coming to the temple who are celebrating special occasions by completing eternally binding ordinances on behalf of deceased family members. These faithful Saints find tremendous joy in performing this wonderful service, and they are filled with a great spirit of love that becomes a connecting force between them and generations past.

In the temple

we find the perfect laboratory

where we can feel a sense of the divine

as love fills our hearts.

LOVE OF GOD

Since love is the greatest power in the universe and is the greatest characteristic of our Father in Heaven and of the Savior, it is imperative that we go to the temple to prepare us to understand the love of God. Understanding the love of God will enable us to love one another, our spouses, our children, our friends, our neighbors, even our enemies. That understanding can come to us only through the power of the Spirit. In the temple we find the perfect laboratory where we can feel a sense of the divine as love fills our hearts.

∞

Kathleen: One day we received a telephone call informing us that a man in his early forties was being transported to the temple by ambulance, on a gurney. He was a very accomplished young man who was in the final stages of an incurable cancer. This day he was to be sealed to his beautiful wife, who was receiving her own endowment. When we attempted to move him upstairs to the sealing room, we discovered that we could not get his gurney into the elevator, and therefore were required to remove him from the gurney and place him in a wheelchair. This was very precarious because he was on oxygen and in a very weakened condition. When his wife, who was waiting in the celestial room, was told that he was being brought up in a wheelchair, she panicked. "That's impossible!" she said. "He cannot survive in a sitting position."

As he arrived and was wheeled into the sealing room, he looked at his wife and, with tears streaming down his face, he took off the oxygen lines and said, "I have waited so long for this day and will not let anything interfere." Everyone in the room was in tears. We understood that the love he felt for his wife and for God transcended any limitations mortality had placed on him.

The temple is a house of love. We have witnessed that love on a daily basis. We have felt the overwhelming power of the love of God. That love has been evidenced in the lives of the workers and patrons in the temple. We have watched the power of God's love fill a troubled soul or mend a broken heart. We have seen the love of God radiate in the eyes of Heavenly Father's children who come to worship in the temple. We have watched as loving servants administered the eternal ordinances of the temple. We have experienced a love as pure as anything we will probably ever feel in mortality.

A letter received from a patron speaks of this love: "I

have been coming to the Salt Lake Temple for nearly two years on a weekly basis. This past year I have mostly been doing an endowment session and have been so touched. It never fails that somewhere during the session someone will pause for only a moment and then proceed with the line, only now it is not a line, it is a testimony of the Savior. That has been my treat each week to feel their testimonies of the Savior while being taught the plan of salvation."

Is it any wonder that the world demeans the power of love and tends to try to redefine it in base and immoral ways? It seems obvious that Satan does everything in his power to fight against God, to attempt to pervert and destroy the purity of the love of God, thus focusing on destroying the most powerful influence from our Heavenly Father, the power of love. It is in the temple that we can understand and be taught the fulness of the power of God's love, and there we can receive covenants that bind us and our families to Him eternally.

⊁ ⊰

What am I doing daily to enable the pure power of love to be a controlling force in my life?

Chapter 3

LOVINGKINDNESS

We have thought of thy lovingkindness,
O God, in the midst of thy temple.

PSALM 48:9

s we prepare ourselves to try to understand the eternal things of our Heavenly Father, the key is to incorporate in our lives the attributes of the Savior as taught in the temple. When the Savior appeared to the Nephites, He challenged His disciples by asking: "Therefore, what manner of men ought ye to be? Verily I say unto you, even as I am" (3 Nephi 27:27).

When we attended the New Temple Presidents Seminar prior to the beginning of our service, we heard members of the First Presidency and other General Authorities use the word *lovingkindness.* This piqued our curiosity, and one night, following a day of instruction, we pulled out our scriptures and began to research the word. We discovered that in the Old Testament it is one word, but in the other books of scripture it appears as two words. It became clear that in the scriptures of the Old Testament, the single word *lovingkindness* is in itself an attribute often connected with the Lord Himself. For example: "But let him that glorieth glory in this, that he understandeth and knoweth me, that I am the Lord which exercise lovingkindness, judgment, and righteousness, in the earth: for in these things I delight, saith the Lord" (Jeremiah 9:24).

The prophet Isaiah also spoke of this attribute of the Lord: "I will mention the lovingkindnesses of the Lord, and the praises of the Lord, according to all that the Lord hath bestowed on us, and the great goodness toward the house of Israel, which he hath bestowed on them according to his mercies, and according to the multitude of his loving-kindesses" (Isaiah 63:7).

We also realized that *lovingkindness* is an action word that, when incorporated into our lives, will draw us closer to Deity: "And they shall mention the loving kindness of their Lord, and all that he has bestowed upon them according to

Lovingkindness *is an action word*

that, when incorporated into our lives,

will draw us closer to Deity.

his goodness, and according to his loving kindness, forever and ever" (D&C 133:52).

As we studied this word, we were drawn to Psalm 48:9, where David in his praise for the Lord said: "We have thought of thy lovingkindness, O God, in the midst of thy temple." We recognized that we were in the midst of His temple and that we should reflect this great attribute of the Savior. This word spoke to us, and we began to use and teach the importance of lovingkindness to those who served in the temple. We noticed that those whose actions reflected lovingkindness were more easily open to the prompting of the Spirit. Patrons were drawn to them, and a wonderful feeling of warmth and love resulted. The feelings generated by this understanding brought great blessings into many lives.

∞

Richard: One Sunday morning the temple recorder got a call from a young bride and groom. They had been married in the temple the prior week and were leaving for their honeymoon on Monday morning. They had suddenly realized that they had failed to request and acquire the proper documentation of their wedding, which verified the legal change of the bride's name. They were in a panic and pleaded for help with a solution. A call was placed to the sister who supervises the marriage records, and without hesitation, she volunteered to drive several miles from her home to the temple. She copied the records and then personally delivered them to this choice young couple. The great example shown by this faithful temple worker not only relieved the worried couple and saved their honeymoon but set a beautiful model of lovingkindness. That spirit of lovingkindness prevails among those who work in the temple and should be manifest in the lives of all who follow the Savior. It is also apparent that people who incorporate this Christlike attribute in their lives become more receptive to the spiritual teachings of the temple.

Kathleen: Another worker recalled a patron she met who was very gruff and unfriendly. When this woman came to the temple, she never smiled, never even lifted her head to greet others, nor did she ever speak to anyone. This patron continued to come on a weekly basis, bringing with her each week her "sour countenance." The worker decided that she would take it upon herself to reach out to this patron with lovingkindness, regardless of how the patron reacted. Week after week as the patron arrived, the worker extended a warm and cheery greeting.

We can return our thanks to the Lord

by accomplishing the work in the temple

that He has commanded us to do.

After several weeks the patron began to respond, making eye contact and finally even offering a smile. As time went on they became friends, calling each other by name and exchanging pleasantries. Lovingkindness penetrated both of their hearts, and the total countenance of the patron changed. Yes, lovingkindness is an attribute of the Savior, and when we incorporate this great attribute into our lives, not only do we change, but those around us are also changed.

⬯

During the wedding rush of June a young bride wrote this simple statement, sharing thoughts that reflected her gratitude for the lovingkindness she had experienced in the temple:

"Dear Temple Sisters,

"I just wanted to thank you for helping to make my wedding day such a beautiful day. The sisters were all so helpful and sweet and truly took care of our every need! I felt so beautiful and special and like I was truly in heaven. I had always planned on and prepared for a temple marriage but I wanted you to know that it was more wonderful than I could have hoped it would be thanks in part to your selfless service. I love you all and hope to see you again (in this life or the next)."

As the temple workers embraced the principle of lovingkindness, their love for their service, for the other workers, for the patrons, and for the Lord increased. Even the patrons began to notice this. This attribute of lovingkindness was contagious. Patrons responded by expressing gratitude for the lovingkindness extended to them by the workers.

There are an innumerable number of ways in which we can incorporate lovingkindness into our lives. They are very simple but they affect us in remarkable ways. They include such ordinary phrases as "I'm sorry," "Please forgive me," "Thank you," "May I help you?" "I'd be happy to!" When combined with similar actions, they build a framework for lovingkindness in our lives.

We live in the dispensation of the fulness of times, when the gospel of Jesus Christ in its fulness has been restored to the earth. God has demonstrated His lovingkindness by establishing temples throughout the world. People across the earth who never dreamed of having access to a temple now enjoy the blessings of temple worship in their own lands. This great gift of temples has opened the door to eternal blessings that in times past have not been easily accessible. With that gift comes a responsibility. We can return our thanks to the Lord by accomplishing the work in the temple that He has commanded us to do. Thereby, we will assist in the fulfillment of the Savior's mission "to bring to pass the immortality and eternal life of man" (Moses 1:39). It is our ultimate act of lovingkindness to provide for our ancestors the binding eternal ordinances of salvation. In return, through the Lord's lovingkindness, our lives are blessed and magnified.

+‡‡‡‡+

What do I do to demonstrate lovingkindness in all my personal relationships?

Chapter 4

REVERENCE THE
HOUSE OF THE LORD

Put off thy shoes from off thy feet, for the place
whereon thou standest is holy ground.

EXODUS 3:5

Two days prior to beginning our service as president and matron of the Salt Lake Temple, we took the occasion to walk through the temple at a time when no one else was there. We started in the basement and slowly made our way up, sometimes opening doors and finding places we had never seen. As we walked through the temple, we talked of those who sacrificed so much to build this holy edifice. Many of them hardly had roofs over their heads, and yet they gave all they had because they knew it was to be the house of the Lord. Many times we were overcome with emotion as we thought of the sacrifice and vision of those early Saints. We were awed with the exquisite craftsmanship throughout the building. There came into our hearts on that day a deep reverence for and an understanding of whose house it is. It was not long into our service that we recognized the Lord was in charge and we were merely His vehicle.

That feeling of reverence and awe never subsided. It grew day by day, and the thrill of spending time in His holy house only increased as time passed and as our reverence and love for the Lord grew.

But you don't have to be the president or matron of a temple to experience this kind of reverence for the Lord's holy house. This feeling of reverence and awe comes to each person who absorbs the sacredness of those holy surroundings and attunes his or her thoughts and feelings to the beauty of the temple. Every temple is built with strict attention to the quality and intricate detail of every part therein. Each evidences a magnificent effort of labor and sacrifice. So many have given so much so that we may be blessed through our worship in these wonderful houses of the Lord. Elder J. Golden Kimball said: "Every stone in it [the Salt Lake Temple] is a sermon to me. It tells of suffering, it tells of sacrifice, it preaches—every rock in it, preaches a discourse. When it was dedicated, it seemed to me that it was the greatest sermon that has ever been preached since the Sermon on the Mount. . . . Every window, every steeple, everything about the Temple speaks of the things of God, and gives evidence of the faith of the people who built it" (in Conference Report, April 1915, 79).

We witnessed the effect of reverence on a daily basis in the lives of those who served in the temple and those who came to the temple to worship. We quickly recognized that in the temple, *reverence* is an action verb. As President Marion G. Romney taught: "My dictionary defines *reverence* as 'profound respect mingled with love and devotion.' When we speak of reverence with respect to God, this reverence and respect, mingled with love and devotion, takes on the quality of worshipful adoration. Reverence may be measured, I think, by the quality of one's veneration for the object of his reverence. If this be true, then the more one loves God, the deeper will be his reverence for Him. . . .

"To be quiet in church is, of course, something that goes along with reverence, but being quiet is not in itself reverence. However, when one recognizes the house in which he is meeting as the dwelling place of the Lord, whom he loves with all his heart, then it is not difficult for him to have reverence for it" ("Reverence," 3, 4).

As we take upon ourselves the attitude of profound reverence for the Lord, it brings about a change in our minds, in our hearts. This reverence is radiated through our countenance. It brings a smile to our face and a warmth to our spirit, which in turn influences our actions and reaches out to those around us. Numerous studies have shown conclusively that smiling is contagious and directly affects both ourselves and others who see us. Reverence is also contagious, and it affects both ourselves and those around us. A reverent spirit is a happy spirit, and, in the Lord's house, that spirit is developed and magnified and purified.

One of the workers expressed her feelings of reverence for the temple in this way: "I take the light-rail train to the temple every Tuesday so I can ride home with my husband, who comes to the temple from work. As I am walking up Main Street, I always look up to the magnificent house of the Lord. And two things come to my mind: 'Here we will build a temple to our God,' and 'Never lose the thrill of coming to the temple.' I always ponder those two things as I walk toward my evening of service in His holy house. And my heart is filled with enthusiasm and anticipation as I enter those doors every Tuesday afternoon."

Nowhere in the world but in the temple do you find hundreds of people who are willing to give so much of their

A reverent spirit is a happy spirit,

and, in the Lord's house,

that spirit is developed

and magnified and purified.

time and effort to serve long hours, without monetary compensation, because of the reverence they feel for the Lord's work. It is that reverence that motivates their dedication. It is through this ongoing process of acting in accordance with our reverent feelings that the Holy Spirit may teach and may ultimately become our constant companion.

Another worker expressed her feelings of reverence in this way: "One quiet morning, shortly after I started to work in the temple, the supervisor asked if I'd like to go work in the laundry. As I stepped into that room I instantly felt such a beautiful spirit. There was clean laundry neatly stacked everywhere, washers and dryers quietly running, large bins labeled 'clean' or 'soiled.' There were a couple of sisters working on sewing machines, large folding tables just the right size for standing and folding. The room was bright, and everything was hushed and well organized.

"However, what instantly impressed me the most was the sweet, quiet reverence that met me there. The sisters spoke softly as they greeted me warmly. My first impression was that, even in the laundry, reverence prevails. I love these sisters! The love they have for what they do is eminent. They reverence their calling. They reverence the house of the Lord."

Elder D. Todd Christofferson said: "When you develop

a deepening reverence for sacred things, the Holy Spirit becomes your frequent and then constant companion. You grow in understanding and truth" ("Sense of the Sacred," 31).

In D&C 50:24 the Lord teaches us: "That which is of God is light; and he that receiveth light, and continueth in God, receiveth more light; and that light groweth brighter and brighter until the perfect day." Have you ever had a perfect day in the temple? Do you stand in awe of what is available to you in His holy house?

∞

Richard: One day early in our service I was walking through the temple to get acquainted with the workers. I went into the laundry and saw an elderly woman sitting at a mangle iron pressing temple clothing. Her shoulders were bent, her fingers were gnarled, her hair was gray, and it was apparent that she was well along in years. As I approached her I asked her how long she had been performing this service. She looked at me with tears in her eyes and said, "I have been doing this for twenty-six years and I absolutely love it!"

I stood in awe that day. Here was a woman who for so many years had done this tedious labor, and yet it was

Developing an attitude of reverence

in our lives will open the spiritual channels

of communication in the temple.

obvious that her heart was filled with reverence and love, knowing that she was serving in the house of the Lord.

Each day she came to the temple was a perfect day for her.

∞

The temple is an oasis in the world. It removes us from the noise, the clamor, the clutter and turmoil of the world. It opens a laboratory of spirituality that leads us to inspiration and revelation.

∞

Kathleen: Some time ago, we walked into the celestial room of the temple and there found a wonderful young couple from Africa sitting with tears in their eyes as they tried to absorb the beauty of that room. They were in Utah to get their respective degrees at the university. Their children were still in Africa, and they hadn't seen them for more than a year. They shared how they had found the gospel and had been baptized one year before. This day they had come to the temple for the first time. They sweetly expressed their love of Heavenly Father and their gratitude for the eternal ordinances they had received. They were overwhelmed with the beauty and exquisite workmanship of the temple and the deep reverence they felt for our Heavenly Father and this beautiful house of the Lord. The humility and reverence that radiated from this couple will never be forgotten.

∞

President Boyd K. Packer, in a talk aptly titled "Reverence Invites Revelation," said this: "The world grows increasingly noisy. Clothing and grooming and conduct are looser and sloppier. . . . Irreverence suits the purposes of the adversary by obstructing the delicate channels of revelation in both mind and spirit."

He concluded his remarks: "In the spirit of reverence, I bear testimony that God lives, that Jesus is the Christ, that the Holy Ghost—our comforter, our teacher—will come to us if we will maintain a spirit of reverence" ("Reverence Invites Revelation," 22–23).

Reverence is absolutely essential in our temple worship. Developing an attitude of reverence in our lives will open the spiritual channels of communication in the temple.

+≁≁+

How can I leave the world outside and enter the temple with an attitude of reverence for the house of the Lord?

Part 2

HOW TO LEARN IN
THE TEMPLE

Chapter 5

THE PRINCIPLE, THE SAVIOR, AND ME

And do thou grant, Holy Father, that all those
who shall worship in this house may be taught.

D&C 109:14

D uring our service in the temple and since that time, many people have approached us with the question: "How can I learn and understand what is taught in the temple?" This question precipitated great pondering on our part, and we came to recognize one of the important ways in which we could begin to unlock the understanding of the sacred ordinances of the temple. Our learning thereafter became and continues to be exciting and uplifting.

We recognized that this Church was restored because a young boy went to the Lord and asked the question,

"Which church is true?" Throughout his prophetic mission, he received many revelations from the Lord, and most came because a question was asked and the answer was given.

Asking questions holds the key to unlocking and understanding the symbolic teachings of the temple. So often when we were serving in the temple we were asked to explain certain aspects of the temple ordinances. People were seeking our interpretation. The problem was, they were asking the wrong source.

An understanding of the eternal truths that are taught in the temple comes in personal ways by searching, pondering, praying, and asking our Heavenly Father the questions that will unlock the knowledge we seek. And then, as our hearts are prepared, our minds will be opened.

In our quest to find this greater understanding, we developed a little formula that we call "The Principle, the Savior, and Me." It is a bit like a "connect-the-dots" puzzle, and it involves three steps that are easy to apply.

Step 1. When you sit in the temple—any part of the temple, including the baptistry—listen carefully for the doctrinal principles that are being taught. You will find that almost every sentence used in administering the ordinances of the temple contains a doctrinal principle.

Step 2. Once you have identified the principle, ask

Asking questions holds the key

to unlocking and understanding

the symbolic teachings of the temple.

yourself, "How does this principle relate to the Savior?" remembering that everything taught in the temple relates directly to the Savior, His divinity, and His Atonement.

Step 3. Then ask yourself, "What does this mean to me, and how do I apply it in my life?"

If you will use this little formula, your understanding can be enlarged as the Spirit teaches the things of God. Following are some examples that will help you get started.

Step 1. The Principle: There is a fundamental principle that we learn at an early age. It is taught in the first Primary song most of us learn to sing. It is this: *I am a child of God, and as such I am individually important to my Heavenly Father.* This principle is taught both in the temple and in the scriptures.

Think of the baptistry. In the Salt Lake Temple, there are approximately 447,000 baptisms for the dead completed each year. When those baptisms are performed, wouldn't it save a lot of time if, when you stood in the water, the officiator read off 10 names or 50 or 100 names and then immersed you in the water? If he did this, the work would go so much faster and be so much more efficient.

But that is not the Lord's way. Those baptisms—indeed, all the ordinances in the temple—are done for one person at a time. What does that tell you? It teaches that we are individually important to Heavenly Father. That is the principle.

Step 2. The Savior: Now we ask, "How does this principle relate to the Savior?" The Savior so loved us as individuals that He was willing to suffer and die and atone for our sins in order that we might return to our Father in Heaven. We are convinced that His love for each of us is so great that if somehow His Atonement had missed one of us, He would come back and do it all over again because we are so important to Him.

Step 3. And Me: What does this mean to me and how do I use this in my life? This principle tells us that our Heavenly Father knows each of us and considers us each a child of great worth. He hears our prayers. He knows our thoughts. He knows our hearts. He knows our needs. He loves us and blesses us as we live in accordance with His teachings. As Jesus taught the Nephites, "Your Father knoweth what things ye have need of before ye ask him" (3 Nephi 13:8). That knowledge can give us greater determination to serve Him.

Another example:

Step 1. The Principle: Men and women are created to be different—by design.

Again, this principle is taught both in the temple and

in the scriptures. Remember the story of Adam and Eve being tempted by Lucifer. Lucifer knew of their differences and used them to try to accomplish his purposes. When he tempted Adam, he appealed to his intellect—suggesting that if he partook of the fruit it would make him *wise*.

When he approached Eve, he used words that appealed to her sensitivities as a woman—words such as *delicious* and *desirable*. "When the woman saw that the tree was *good* for food, and that it became *pleasant* to the eyes, and a tree to be *desired* to make her *wise*, she took of the fruit thereof, and did eat" (Moses 4:12; emphasis added).

Eve, with her nurturing qualities, remembered that she and Adam had been commanded to multiply and replenish the earth. Her understanding of this important mission led her to partake, and the law of the Lord was fulfilled.

Step 2. Now ask: "How does this relate to the Savior?"

The fall was necessary to bring to pass the immortality and eternal life of man. That act brought forth the need for a Redeemer and Savior and put into place the entire plan of salvation.

Step 3. Then ask yourself: "How does this apply to me?"

Instead of resisting our differences, we ought to embrace them, use them, and rejoice in them. They have been given to us for a purpose. When we put them together, they make a whole. Remember, when Adam and Eve left the garden they went hand in hand, side by side. She was not lagging behind him feeling ashamed and guilty, and he was not chastising her for landing them in a world full of trials and hard work!

When we understand that the difference between men and women is divinely given, we don't let those differences turn into a war. Instead, we use them to accomplish common goals. This principle is true not only in a marriage but in any relationship—on a committee, in a ward council, in your home, in the workplace, and in any social setting.

One final example:

Step 1. The Principle: We have power over Satan.

This principle is also taught in both the temple and the scriptures. Moses understood this principle and invoked that power when Satan attempted to deceive him, claiming that he, Satan, was God, and commanding Moses to worship him: "Nevertheless, calling upon God, [Moses] received strength, and he commanded, saying: Depart from me, Satan, for this one God only will I worship, which is the God of glory" (Moses 1:20).

Step 2. Ask, "How does this relate to the Savior?" The Savior voluntarily accepted our Heavenly Father's plan for our eternal salvation. He did it knowing He would have to

As you embark on your own quest

to understand the principles taught in the temple,

you will find new knowledge opening to you

and will further understand that the temple

ordinances define the pathway of life.

overcome the temptations of Satan, suffer for our sins, and bring about the Atonement. In so doing, He gained absolute dominion over Satan as our Redeemer and Savior.

Step 3. Now ask yourself, "How does this apply to me?" Because of the Savior's sacrifice, each of us is given the promise that if we obey the commandments, Satan cannot control us. We have to sin to open our hearts to Satan's power. We even have, through the priesthood, the power to rebuke the adversary.

By applying these three steps, we have a formula for unlocking our understanding of the great symbolism in the eternal teachings of the temple.

The three examples above are only a beginning. As you embark on your own quest to understand the principles taught in the temple, you will find new knowledge opening to you and will further understand that the temple ordinances define the pathway of life. They help us understand how we can find happiness and ultimately return to our Heavenly Father to live in His presence eternally.

The Lord made this clear in D&C 124:55: "I command you again to build a house to my name . . . that you may prove yourselves unto me that ye are faithful in all things whatsoever I command you, that I may bless you, and crown you with honor, immortality, and eternal life."

The temple truly is a house of learning. By using this process, we can begin to identify the principles taught in the temple, understand how they apply to the Savior, and see how, if effectively used, they will change our lives.

If we will, with desire and dedication, embark on a quest for learning in the holy temple, the Lord will teach us by helping us understand the way to open the power of godliness and define the pathway to our personal exaltation. "And this greater priesthood administereth the gospel and holdeth the key of the mysteries of the kingdom, even the key of the knowledge of God. Therefore, in the ordinances thereof, the power of godliness is manifest. And without the ordinances thereof, and the authority of the priesthood, the power of godliness is not manifest unto men in the flesh" (D&C 84:19–21).

Since our release, we continue to visit many different temples. Although the structures are very different, the feeling and the teachings are the same. By using the simple formula—The Principle, the Savior, and Me—we have found that we enter the temple with greater excitement and searching. At times we find that we are almost on the edge of our seats because we are listening so intently and with such purpose. Each time we agree that we will each search for a new principle that we have not yet identified. Without fail, on every visit, we have identified a new principle. In our minds we relate it to the Savior and then ask how it applies to our own life. When we complete our session, and before we leave the temple, we sit together and relate what we have discovered.

∞

Kathleen: One day I went to the temple feeling somewhat discouraged because of the struggle of trying to organize our home after three years of imposed neglect. Weeks and weeks of cleaning drawers, organizing files, sorting junk, and rearranging closet space were beginning to wear on me. It seemed that the more I did, the more there was to do. The task looked endless. On that day as I sat in the temple with a desire to learn, it suddenly opened up to me. The Lord Himself had been through the process of creating, organizing, sorting, and arranging this world. He did it step by step, one day at a time. At the close of each day He took joy in His accomplishments and left tomorrow's tasks for tomorrow. I was so excited that I could hardly wait to share this new insight with my husband, who had been listening for some time to my complaints and discouragement. I returned to my tasks with new insight and energy. They no longer seemed mundane, but a process in which I could take joy and find satisfaction in my accomplishments. It was a great learning experience and an exciting day for me.

Applying our learning formula has been a remarkable experience. It has assisted us to be alert with excitement and to be taught marvelous spiritual truths that give personal guidance and often provide answers to the struggles of our lives. The temple is truly a remarkable house of learning.

How can I make the temple a house of learning that will give direction to my life?

Chapter 6

A PLACE OF PERSONAL
REVELATION

If thou shalt ask, thou shalt receive revelation
upon revelation, knowledge upon knowledge, that thou
mayest know the mysteries and peaceable things—that
which bringeth joy, that which bringeth life eternal.

D&C 42:61

Kathleen: One day a patron who greeted me in the temple said, "Oh it must be so wonderful to spend so much time in the temple. I bet you have had lots of visions."

I thought about that for some time. I had never had a vision, in the context of the way we usually define visions. And I realized that I did not seek a vision, nor did I need a vision, because every day I spent in the temple I had thoughts and feelings confirm to me that the Lord is mindful of each one of us and of our presence in His house.

∞

In the Doctrine and Covenants, the Lord counseled the Prophet Joseph and Oliver Cowdery, who were in the process of translating the Book of Mormon. The Lord instructed them in the process of personal revelation, saying: "Yea, behold, I will tell you in your mind and in your heart, by the Holy Ghost, which shall come upon you and which shall dwell in your heart. Now, behold, this is the spirit of revelation" (D&C 8:2–3).

We can receive personal revelation in the temple if we pay attention to the thoughts that come to us and the feelings we experience in our hearts.

∞

Kathleen: One day I received a letter from a patron that said, in part, "I married a wonderful man who is not a member of the Church. We have had a wonderful and blessed marriage of almost twenty-three years. Five healthy and obedient children have been added to

We can receive personal revelation in the temple

if we pay attention to the thoughts that come

to us and the feelings we experience in our hearts.

that happiness. But I have traversed a unique path of membership in the kingdom with a nonmember spouse. Although he has always supported my activity in the Church and that of our children . . . he has been reluctant to embrace membership in the Church.

"A year ago, our oldest daughter found herself in a serious and very dangerous relationship. She was engaged to a member of a polygamist family and was quickly turning away from our family and the Church. I felt like my husband and I had exhausted all our abilities to reach her. It was in this state of mind that I attended our stake temple day.

"I began the day participating in baptisms and confirmations. I then attended an endowment session. As I pleaded with the Lord for help with my daughter, the thought occurred to me that the one thing I might say to her that could cause her pause in her current course would be, 'What will we do when our family is ready to go to the temple to be sealed as an eternal family, and you are not with us?' That thought soon led to doubt, as I could not say with assurance that our family would arrive at that day in this life.

"Later in the day I was overcome with a rush of gratitude in my heart as I recognized the Lord was mindful of me and of my pleadings.

"I did have the conversation with my daughter about how we would encounter a bittersweet day in the temple sealing room without her. I hoped she could feel my confidence. She found the strength to end that relationship a few months later and is now engaged to a tremendous young man who is a member of the Church.

"I would end the story there, but it would omit the very best part. Last week, after nearly a year of learning the gospel through the love and patience of eight dedicated sister missionaries, my husband has finally arrived at a baptismal date."

This is a woman who paid attention to the feelings of her heart and the thoughts that came into her mind. In other words, she received personal revelation while in the temple. As a result, the Lord was able to guide her through a difficult time and bless her family.

∞

Elder John A. Widtsoe taught: "The endowment which was given by revelation can best be understood by revelation;

and to those who seek most vigorously, with pure hearts, will the revelation be the greatest. I believe the busy person on the farm, in the shop, in the office, or in the household, who has his worries and troubles, can solve his problems better and more quickly in the house of the Lord than anywhere else" ("Temple Worship," 63).

Isn't it amazing that the Lord would bestow upon each of us the magnificent gift and promise of personal revelation. It is so personal in nature that it is not shared or duplicated in any other human being. It speaks to the fact that the Lord loves us and knows us intimately, as individuals. We are important in His plan, and our personal well-being is His concern, and the temple is a center of learning and personal revelation. It is there for us to receive if we do our part.

Elder Gerald N. Lund stated: "The voice of the Spirit is described as still and small and one that whispers. How can a voice be still? Why is it likened to a whisper? Because the Spirit almost always speaks to our minds and to our hearts rather than to our ears" ("Opening Our Hearts," 32).

∞

Richard: A thirteen-year-old boy whose family was moving to a new home had to decide if he wanted to change schools or remain where he was. He knew he could argue it both ways. Staying in his old school felt safe and comfortable, but going to the new school would bring new friends and a place in his neighborhood. He agonized over this for many days and then decided he needed to go to the temple. The following morning his mother dropped him off at the baptistry. During the course of the morning, he thought about his decision. He weighed the pros and cons. When his mother picked him up, he told her he had decided to go to the new school. In answer to her questions, he said that while he was in the temple, he just felt good about it.

∞

As President Boyd K. Packer has said: "The Holy Ghost speaks with a voice that you *feel* more than you *hear*" ("Personal Revelation," 60; emphasis in original).

∞

Richard: One afternoon the temple recorder received a call from a sister who said her husband had been recently diagnosed with liver cancer and had been given two weeks to live. They had contacted their six adult children and spouses and were assembling them for the weekend. One son was serving in the United States Navy.

His ship had just docked and he was able to secure leave in order to return home. The youngest daughter had a mission call and was scheduled to enter the Missionary Training Center two weeks hence.

This sister said that the family was planning to be together in the temple the following Tuesday morning and would be on the 5:45 A.M. session. The recorder assured them they would be welcomed.

Tuesday morning, the family arrived as planned and prepared for the session. As they sat together in that holy house, the emotions of the family and of all those present were evident. They had gathered, dressed in white, prepared to partake of the sacred temple ordinances.

At the conclusion of the endowment ceremony, they sat together in a small room, where they were left alone to talk and share their feelings.

As they prepared to leave, that dear mother said, "I don't know what is going to happen to us, but I do know the Lord is mindful of us and of our great love for each other and for Him. Somehow, with the Lord's help, we will get through this." They felt the kind of peace and comforting spirit that comes only from a loving Heavenly

Father. For them, this was personal revelation—the kind of revelation that brings comfort in time of need.

∞

In the three years that we served in the temple, we never once heard of anyone who had a vision. Nor did we ever see anyone leave with a detailed list of "dos and don'ts" that would answer all problems and cure all ills. The Lord does not usually answer our prayers by giving us visions or by handing us a to-do list. But He does answer our prayers. And He prompts us in many ways.

Sometimes a prompting comes from hearing just a line or even a word in a new way. Sometimes it comes in a calming feeling of peace. Sometimes it comes in the form of ideas that come to our minds and hearts. Sometimes it comes in an expansion of our understanding of the principles taught in the ordinances. At times it may come from observing others. But it can and will come as we prepare our minds and hearts to be in tune with the Spirit that gives revelation and light.

∞

Kathleen: One day an ordinance worker in the temple came to work her shift. She had been wrestling with a decision regarding her employment. She was

The Lord does not usually answer our prayers

by giving us visions or by handing us

a to-do list. But He does answer our prayers.

assigned that day to follow an endowment session. While sitting in the ordinance room and listening to the dialogue, a sentence that she had heard hundreds of times suddenly lit up in her mind like a neon sign. It was the answer to her dilemma. With great joy she recognized that she had received personal revelation. This had come to her in an unexpected moment and in an unexpected way. Because she was in tune with the Spirit, her mind and her heart were enlightened, and the solution to her problem became clear.

∽

Nephi taught: "When a man speaketh by the power of the Holy Ghost the power of the Holy Ghost carrieth it unto the hearts of the children of men" (2 Nephi 33:1).

One temple patron expressed it this way: "Sometimes when I am participating in the ordinances of the temple, the worker performing a particular part does so in such a spiritual way that I feel as though I have been taught by the very person whose part is being portrayed. It is at these times that I feel the power of the doctrine, and of how it applies to my life."

Elder David A. Bednar explains: "Please notice how the power of the Spirit carries the message *unto* but not necessarily *into* the heart. . . . Ultimately . . . the content of a message and the witness of the Holy Ghost penetrate into the heart only if a receiver allows them to enter" ("Seek Learning by Faith," 61; emphasis in original).

The Lord confirmed this understanding to the Prophet Joseph Smith: "Therefore, why is it that ye cannot understand and know, that he that receiveth the word by the Spirit of truth receiveth it as it is preached by the Spirit of truth? Wherefore, he that preacheth and he that receiveth, understand one another, and both are edified and rejoice together" (D&C 50:21–22).

The Lord has made temples available to each of us wherein, if our hearts are prepared and we are listening, the Holy Ghost will give us personal revelation through the thoughts that come into our minds and the feelings that come into our hearts.

How can I prepare my mind and heart to hear and recognize the revelations of the Lord?

Chapter 7

SEEING YOURSELF AS
THE LORD SEES YOU

[God] knows all thy thoughts, and thou seest that thy
thoughts are made known unto us by his Spirit.

ALMA 12:3

Sometimes we allow the world and its challenges and trials not only to define us but to limit our vision of who we really are. In the temple the Lord provides for us a pure atmosphere, shielded from the world, where we can rescue the understanding that we are literally children of our Heavenly Father.

Kathleen: One afternoon a young woman sought me out and shared this experience. She said that for a time in her life, she attended the temple on a weekly basis, but because all was not well with her, she began to blame the Lord and felt that perhaps she was not worthy or that the Lord was not pleased with her in some way, so she quit going. But life did not get better. In fact, it got worse. In the midst of some deep soul-searching, she determined she would try going back to the temple.

That first time back she was apprehensive, not knowing how she would feel. But while she was there, something happened. She couldn't really identify what it was but she said she just felt better. She began to feel like a person again and had renewed energy. Since that time her days have improved. As we talked, she suggested that maybe she was beginning to see herself as the Lord sees her instead of letting the world define who she is.

∽

The world has a way of telling us who we are and what we are worth. We often underestimate our own potential and power because we get caught up in things that are not important—that in fact are detrimental to our growth and progress.

We often underestimate

our own potential and power

because we get caught up in things

that are not important.

⚭

Kathleen: One day I sat with a woman who had been serving in a leadership position in the temple for three years. As we visited, she told me that when she accepted the calling she was terrified. She had come to this calling with no previous leadership experience. Her husband was not a member of the Church, and although he was supportive, he understood little of what such a calling would require.

And so it was with great trepidation that she accepted the call and went to work. She labored long and hard, feeling inadequate and ill prepared. But she said that when she finally changed her attitude from "I can't do this" to "I can do this with the Lord's help," she found not only great satisfaction but success in her labors. She served well, conducting meetings, training other workers, and handling difficult problems. She had soared, and her testimony of the Lord had expanded. And then she made this wonderful and very enlightening statement: "Because of this experience I have learned that the Lord can make something out of nothing."

Here was a woman who once saw herself as nothing, but when she let the Lord work in her life, she began to see herself as the Lord saw her. It was exciting!

∞

Life is full of discouragement and difficulties. It can be downright hard. And it takes its toll on each of us. We all have times when we feel inadequate or useless or incapable or even worthless.

∞

Kathleen: There were days in the temple when I would get discouraged. It seemed that the faster I worked, the farther behind I got. I could not seem to cover all the bases and meet all the demands that were placed on me. One day, I had the need to leave the temple and return several times. Each time required a change of clothes. I would change from street clothes to temple clothes to street clothes to temple clothes over and over. Late in the day, as I was changing clothes for the *eighth time*, I felt frustrated and overwhelmed. Because of the running back and forth, I was behind in my work. I had not taken care of things I thought needed attention. One last time, I pulled my clothes over my head and turned to look in the mirror. As I did, I had one of those miniscule flashes that comes and goes instantaneously but speaks volumes. I saw myself standing in white in the Lord's house, trying to do my best, and the thought came to me: "It does not matter to the Lord if you do not get through the paperwork today, or do not get to the other business of the day. What does matter is that you are here, in His house, serving Him with all your heart. The little things will take care of themselves." I began to weep, and for just a second I think I caught a glimpse of seeing myself as the Lord sees me.

That was a great moment for me, and when I feel myself drowning in the busyness of the world, I try to remember what is really important and ask myself, "Where is my heart? What really matters?"

Richard: One evening Sister Walker and I were preparing for an endowment session. We sat behind the creation room for approximately fifteen minutes waiting for the session to begin. Others who were participating were sitting with us. I noticed one man in particular. It was his first night working in this part of the temple, and he looked terrified, which surprised me, given his background. By the standards of both the world and the Church, he would be considered very accomplished. He had letters behind his name, probably certificates on his wall, and a great deal of experience in his past. But on this night, he sat with head bowed, rehearsing in his mind over and over again the words he was to say. I was struck by the deep humility I saw. I sensed in that moment that I was seeing him as the Lord was seeing him—a humble servant who felt a great desire to serve in a perfect way and was totally dependent upon the Lord for help.

The temple is a "level playing field." Equality prevails. We have often stood near the temple entrance and watched patrons streaming into the temple. Some are dressed in suits and dresses, some in western attire, some in Polynesian muumuus, and some in the colorful attire of African nations. People tend to make judgments of others based on the clothes they are wearing, their hairstyles, or other unusual features. However, when we enter into the house of the Lord, we all clothe ourselves in the same beautiful white clothing, and the artificial judgments of the world disappear. We are seen as the Lord sees us. The worldly accolades fall away. The positions we've held, the letters behind our names, the degrees that have been conferred on us, the plaques that hang on our walls, the titles and accomplishments of the world, and even our physical imperfections

When we enter into the house of the Lord,

the artificial judgments of the world

disappear. We are seen as the Lord sees us.

fade as we come together as children of our Father in heaven
to learn and worship in His house.

∞

Richard: One afternoon a young woman came to the
baptistry to participate in baptisms for the dead. When
she was issued the standard baptismal clothing, she asked
if she could have something with long sleeves. She had
large tattoos that covered her arms and were a source of
great embarrassment to her. The sensitive and inspired
worker responded: "My dear, the Lord will not be looking
at your tattoos today, but rather He will be looking at your
heart. Thank you for coming to the temple."

∞

In John, chapter 10, we read the parable of the Good
Shepherd, in which the Savior reminds us that "he that en-
tereth in by the door is the shepherd of the sheep . . . and the
sheep hear his voice: and he calleth his own sheep by name,
and leadeth them out . . . and the sheep follow him. . . . I
am the good shepherd, and know my sheep, and am known
of mine. . . . My sheep hear my voice, and I know them, and
they follow me: And I give unto them eternal life" (John
10:2–4, 14, 27–28).

The great door to the sheepfold may be found through

the door of the temple. There, as we enter in, we are called by name and are taught and led of the Savior in such a way that we will hear His voice and follow Him, with the promise He gave: "I am the light of the world: he that followeth me shall not walk in darkness, but shall have the light of life" (John 8:12).

The Lord does not expect perfection from us in this life, but He does expect us to try hard and to do our very best. He loves us and knows us in ways that we don't even know ourselves. He knows our hearts and the goodness of our souls, and He will enlighten us and help us to become the people He intends us to be, if we will allow Him to tutor us and lead us along the pathway He has defined. He truly sees us as we really are.

<hr />

What can I do to see myself as the Lord sees me?

Chapter 8

RECEIVING A FULNESS
OF THE HOLY GHOST

. . . and the doctrine of the priesthood shall distil
upon thy soul as the dews from heaven.

D&C 121:45

Richard: Recently I had occasion to spend time with
a great young man who does not share our faith. He is
intelligent and well educated, and he has searched in
depth to understand various cultures and religions of the
world. Although he is a clean-living person, he has not
inquired personally to discover the nature of God and
His gospel. During our discussion it became apparent
that this young man relies on his own intellect to make
the decisions in his life. As we discussed the way in which

one can discover God through faith and the power of the Holy Ghost, he stated that he is confident he has the Holy Ghost because he has at times felt things that helped him to do what is right. This opened a discussion regarding the difference between the light of Christ, promptings of the Holy Ghost, and the gift of the Holy Ghost. He then asked, "How can I receive all of the Holy Ghost?"

∞

There are many who would like to think that if you just walk into the temple and decide that today you will be spiritual and feel the direction of the Holy Ghost, it will happen. Not true! The capacity to receive spiritual direction from the Holy Ghost must be developed by living in harmony with the teachings of the Savior. It will result only as we form habits of worthiness, work and seek to feel and understand the spiritual promptings given to us, and then apply them in our lives. In the temple we are taught what we need to do to receive the fulness of the Holy Ghost. Remember, this is not an event, but a process.

When the Prophet Joseph Smith offered the prayer of dedication for the Kirtland Temple on March 27, 1836, he made a written statement that it had been given to him by revelation. That beautiful prayer became the 109th section of the Doctrine and Covenants, and in it, he said: "And do thou grant, Holy Father, that all those who shall worship in this house may be taught words of wisdom . . . ; and that they may grow up in thee, and receive *a fulness of the Holy Ghost*" (D&C 109:14–15; emphasis added).

Note that the Prophet Joseph was speaking of "those who shall worship in this house"—in other words, members of the Church who have temple recommends and have already received the gift of the Holy Ghost. In this prayer he makes it clear that receiving the gift of the Holy Ghost is not enough, but that we must "grow up" in the Lord and receive "a fulness of the Holy Ghost." Through this inspired prayer, we come to understand that there is a difference between receiving the *gift* of the Holy Ghost and receiving a *fulness* of the Holy Ghost. Accordingly, we understand that it is in the temple that we can receive the "fulness." We then must search to understand what we must do in the temple in order to receive a fulness of the Holy Ghost. The prophet tells us that the key given in the temple to allow us to receive the "fulness of the Holy Ghost" is to "grow up in thee."

❧

Richard: A wonderful couple were invited to the temple to be called as ordinance workers. They had an extensive background, including, among other calls, his service as a bishop, stake president, and mission president. His wife had served as president of several auxiliary organizations. During the interview, the wife stated: "Are you aware that my husband cannot memorize? Our mission motto was one sentence long and he couldn't even memorize that." This humble man nodded his head in agreement and said: "That is true, but if the Lord wants me to serve in the temple and memorize all the parts, I will trust in the Lord and I know that He will help me." They both went to work spending many hours studying and trying to memorize. Within a few months we saw this good man commit to memory all of the parts of the temple ordinances and perform them without hesitation. It was a true gift of the Holy Ghost, opened to him through faith, hard work, and commitment.

When Mercy Fielding Thompson received her endowment in May 1842, the Prophet Joseph said to her: "This will bring you out of darkness into marvelous light" (in "Recollections of the Prophet Joseph Smith," 400).

Franklin D. Richards of the Quorum of the Twelve Apostles wrote: "When the spirit prompted [Joseph Smith]

There is a difference between receiving

the gift of the Holy Ghost

and receiving a fulness of the Holy Ghost.

that his life's work was drawing to a close, and when he saw that his earthly days might be ended before the completion of the [Nauvoo] temple—he called a chosen few, and conferred upon them the ordinances of the holy endowments, so that the divine treasures of his mind might not perish from the world with his death" ("Tour of Historic Scenes," 301).

It is clear that the Prophet Joseph Smith understood the overwhelming importance of the temple ordinances to enable each of us to "grow up" in the Lord and receive "a fulness of the Holy Ghost."

In D&C 121:45–46, the Lord taught us of the process required:

"Let thy bowels also be full of charity towards all men, and to the household of faith, and let virtue garnish thy thoughts unceasingly; then shall thy confidence wax strong in the presence of God; and *the doctrine of the priesthood shall distil upon thy soul as the dews from heaven.*

"The Holy Ghost shall be thy constant companion, and thy scepter an unchanging scepter of righteousness and truth; and thy dominion shall be an everlasting dominion, and without compulsory means it shall flow unto thee forever and ever" (emphasis added).

Isn't it fascinating how the Lord uses common language

to teach deep and profound understanding of spiritual things? His promise is that if we meet the required conditions, then the doctrine of the priesthood (including the great symbolic teachings of the temple) will distil upon our souls as the dews from heaven. Why did the Lord use these common words? What are we being taught regarding the process through such images as "distilling" and "dews"?

We learn from the dictionary two important things: first, *distill* is defined as "to fall or materialize in drops or in a fine moisture; to appear slowly or in small quantities at a time," and second, *dew* is "moisture condensed upon the surfaces of cool bodies esp. at night" (*Merriam-Webster's Collegiate Dictionary*, s.v. "distill"; "dew"). In other words, dew forms only if certain conditions of the atmosphere are present, namely: the correct humidity, the right temperature, and a calm atmosphere. If these conditions are not all present, then dew will not form. Applying this imagery as the scripture does, we learn that the doctrine of the priesthood as taught in the temple will distill upon our souls (in drops or small quantities, "line upon line and precept upon precept") as the dews from heaven (only if the proper conditions are present in our lives).

What, then, are the conditions for us to bring about the distillation process? Suppose we were to liken humidity to our thoughts, temperature to our actions, and a calm atmosphere to our hearts. In order for the "dew" to appear, these three conditions must exist: Our thoughts must be clean, our actions must be in harmony with the gospel, and our hearts must be pure. Only then will the doctrine of the priesthood distil upon our souls as the dews from heaven.

In other words, if we will put our lives, our thoughts, our actions, and our hearts in tune with the Lord, and worship the Lord in His holy temple, then step by step, through the gift of the Holy Ghost, the fulness of the Holy Ghost will be "distilled" upon our souls as the dews from heaven, and we will be empowered to open the many "gifts" of the Holy Ghost in our lives.

Richard: Many years ago while serving on active duty in the military, I was serving as a young, new second lieutenant in charge of a survey platoon. We were given an assignment to participate in a field exercise that required my platoon to be at a designated place on the map at 5:00 A.M. to make radio contact with my battalion commander to receive my orders. I had my own jeep equipped with a large radio and a sergeant to drive me. I had been given the frequency by which I was to contact my commander.

Just before 5:00 A.M., I turned on my radio and turned the large dial to the frequency, but all I got was static. I was almost in a panic when the sergeant said: "May I help, Sir? I think you forgot to *fine tune*." He showed me a small dial, which I turned, and immediately the radio adjusted to the right frequency and brought me into full and clear communication with my commander.

We sometimes find ourselves in the same predicament in life. We have been given all the necessary tools and equipment to communicate with our Heavenly Father, but we let conditions in our lives interfere with our *fine tuning*. For this reason the Lord has given us His holy temple, wherein, if our hearts are pure, we can open the channel of communication through the gifts of the Holy Ghost. Then, as the scriptures teach, we may grow up in the Lord and receive a fulness of the Holy Ghost, and the doctrine of the priesthood shall distill upon our souls as the dews from heaven.

How can I live my life in such a way that I can receive a fulness of the Holy Ghost?

Chapter 9

THE TEMPLE—OUR
KEY TO HAPPINESS

Because of the love of God which did dwell in the hearts of the people . . . there could not be a happier people among all the people who had been created by the hand of God.

4 Nephi 1:15–16

Kathleen: One of the sweet privileges a temple matron has is giving instruction to women who attend the temple prior to receiving their own endowment. Usually they come with excitement and anxious anticipation. They are happy to be there and they radiate a kind of innocent love. They generally attend with an escort, most often a member of their family or close friend.

On one particular day, I was a bit distressed to find a sister who looked deeply sad. She was planning on being married a few days later, and her escort was her soon-to-be-mother-in-law, who spoke no English. I was so concerned about this young woman that I asked a worker to find her after the session and bring her to my office before she left the temple that day. Two hours later she sat in front of me. I began by saying, "Tell me about your mother."

She registered a shocked look and asked, "Why?"

"Well," I said, "she wasn't with you today, and I just wondered."

She then began to weep and told me her family had joined the Church many years ago in Mexico. But since then her parents and two brothers had made choices in their lives that prevented them from temple worship. She had ended up at BYU, had met a wonderful young man from Peru, and they were to be married at the end of the week. And through deep sobs she said, "What should be the happiest day of my life will now be laced with deep sadness because none of my family will be with me."

I was so touched by this young girl's emotion that I asked, "Why didn't you go home to Mexico and be married there where you could be with your family and friends?"

She brightened with resolve and said, "Because I know that my eternal happiness will come from the blessings I receive in the temple, and I am willing to forgo momentary happiness for the eternal blessings that await me."

It is remarkable that during the first ten years following the organization of the Church, at a time when the Church was struggling to survive and grow, the Lord commanded the Saints to sacrifice and build temples. Each time they were driven to a new area, one of the first things they were commanded to do was build a temple. It happened in Kirtland, in Independence, in Far West, and in Nauvoo, as the Lord directed in D&C 124:31: "I command you, all ye my saints, to build a house unto me; and I grant unto you a sufficient time to build a house unto me . . . and if you do not these things . . . ye shall be rejected as a church, with your dead, saith the Lord your God."

The Saints did build and dedicate the temple in Kirtland, and in the dedicatory prayer the Prophet Joseph prayed: "For thou knowest that we have done this work through great tribulation; and out of our poverty we have given of our substance to build a house to thy name, that the Son of Man might have a place to manifest himself to his people" (D&C 109:5).

We live in a wild and challenging world. Our lives are full of turbulence and trials, and at times we struggle with adversity, illness, and loss. Life can be so very hard. And yet, we are told that "men are, that they might have joy" (2 Nephi 2:25).

How is this possible? How can we be happy when the world we live in is filled with chaos and evil? Is it possible that true happiness comes from understanding and living the principles taught in the temple? We believe that to be absolutely true. We have seen evidence of it time and time again.

∞

Richard: A sister from Russia, who had been serving for many years as an ordinance worker in the temple, learned that her mother, who was still living in Russia, was very ill and was not expected to live. This sister felt anxious to return to her homeland and tend to her mother until her death. She said good-bye to her husband and promised to return as soon as her mother passed away, which she expected would be very soon. But when

The temple is a haven in the midst of turbulence.

It is peace in the midst of violence.

It is love in the midst of hatred.

the daughter arrived, the mother rallied and began to improve. She lived for four and half years more. During this time, a great distance separated that sister from her husband and from the glorious work in the temple. Her heart longed for both. In order to compensate, she talked to her husband every day by phone, and each night when she retired to her bed, she would repeat in her mind the entire temple endowment ceremony.

This sister could not go in the temple for a time, but the temple was in her. Not only did that sustain her in her absence, but when she returned to the temple she immediately resumed her service with no retraining needed.

She taught us a great lesson. It is not enough for us to be inside the temple. We must get the temple inside us.

∞

The temple becomes the Lord's laboratory wherein we are taught those principles that, if applied in our lives, will lead us to peace and happiness. It is a haven in the midst of turbulence. It is peace in the midst of violence. It is love in the midst of hatred. It is a sanctuary where we can draw close to our Heavenly Father and His Son, Jesus Christ. As we commit ourselves to learning the spiritual meaning of the eternal ordinances of the temple, and then to applying what we learn, we will place our lives on the path that will bring peace and happiness to each of us, regardless of the adversities we face.

THE TEMPLE IS A HOUSE OF PRAYER

In many places in the Doctrine and Covenants, the Lord refers to His temple as a house of prayer. The Prophet prayed: "O Lord God Almighty, hear us in these our petitions, and answer us from heaven, thy holy habitation" (D&C 109:77). It is in the temple that we can most effectively block out the world and approach our Heavenly Father in prayer, knowing that the adversary cannot go there.

☍

Richard: Some time ago a couple who were serving in the temple suffered a terrible tragedy. Their young granddaughter was brutally murdered. Their grief is impossible to understand fully. As we watched them in the months that followed, we frequently saw them smiling through their tears. One day I asked this gentle man, "How can you manage to smile through your tears when you carry such grief in your heart?"

He answered: "I do feel great tragedy and grief, and my heart is heavy, but the smile is a reflection of what I know in my inner core. I come to the temple, and through prayer and service I have come to more fully know the Savior. He has become my friend, and when I am in His holy house, I feel His great love for me. His spirit envelops me, and He hears me. I love being in the temple. It is here that I can feel close to Him and I can smile through my grief."

∞

THE TEMPLE IS A HOUSE OF SAFETY, SECURITY, AND PEACE

A great clue to the importance of the power of temple ordinances was given by the Prophet Joseph when he prayed at the Kirtland Temple dedication: "And we ask thee, Holy Father, that thy servants may go forth from this house armed with thy power, that thy name may be upon them, and thy glory be round about them, and thine angels have charge over them" (D&C 109:22). Understanding and applying the principles taught in the temple is far more than a "feel-good" experience. This understanding comes only through the Spirit. As we continue to learn and apply these eternal principles, we literally become armed with His power, and this will bring safety, security, and peace into our lives.

∞

Kathleen: One Saturday evening a young couple attended an endowment session in the temple. The sister who was assisting on that session noticed them. They radiated a deep love and a sense of togetherness. The sister watched them and was so impressed with the "electricity" she felt between them that she determined to find them after the session and share her feelings. She found them in the celestial room with heads bowed. She waited for some time, and when they finally looked up, she approached them. She told them that she had been watching them and was moved by the tender love they seemed to demonstrate toward one another. She then noticed the young man's short hair, and it dawned on her. "Are you military?" she asked.

"Yes, ma'am!" he answered.

And then she said, "Are you perchance being deployed?"

"Yes, ma'am. Eight A.M. Monday morning I ship out to Iraq."

The young wife then spoke up. "When he received his orders, we were devastated and terrified. We talked and fasted and prayed. We clung to each other. In our prayerful searching, we were drawn to the temple, seeking a place of safety and help. It is so wonderful to know that while we are separated, the eternal blessings of the temple will connect us. We feel safe and secure here, and having found peace, we know that we can face the challenges that lie ahead."

President Boyd K. Packer taught: "Our labors in the temple cover us with a shield and a protection, both individually and as a people." He also noted: "The Lord will bless us as we attend to the sacred ordinance work of the temples. Blessings there will not be limited to our temple service. We will be blessed in all of our affairs. We will be eligible to have the Lord take an interest in our affairs both spiritual and temporal" (*The Holy Temple,* 265, 182).

THE TEMPLE IS A HOUSE OF LEARNING

The Prophet Joseph prayed: "And do thou grant, Holy Father, that all those who shall worship in this house may be taught words of wisdom out of the best books, and that they may seek learning even by study, and also by faith" (D&C 109:14).

In previous chapters we have taught how to identify doctrinal principles, how to receive personal revelation, and how to prepare our hearts to be tuned to the things of the Spirit. So often the Lord uses the things we do and hear in the temple to answer our personal prayers. One brother who came to the temple for the first time expressed his feelings this way: "Before coming to the temple, I worried and stressed over what it would be like. I asked myself, would I be able to understand what is taught in the temple, or would I be overwhelmed and confused? After coming, I found that what is taught is so beautiful and clear. I know that I have much to learn, and I have a long ways to go, but I am excited at the prospect."

Answers come in unexpected ways and at unexpected times if we are prepared. The Savior promised us: "Ask, and it shall be given you; seek, and ye shall find; knock, and it shall be opened unto you" (Matthew 7:7). Our responsibility is to search and ponder and learn as we worship in the temple.

So often the Lord uses

the things we do and hear in the temple

to answer our personal prayers.

THE TEMPLE IS A HOUSE OF GOD

Again in the Kirtland Temple dedicatory prayer, the Prophet pleaded: "That thy glory may rest down upon thy people, and upon this thy house, which we now dedicate to thee, that it may be sanctified and consecrated to be holy, and that thy holy presence may be continually in this house;

"And that all people who shall enter upon the threshold of the Lord's house may feel thy power, and feel constrained to acknowledge that thou hast sanctified it, and that it is thy house, a place of thy holiness" (D&C 109:12–13).

∞

Kathleen: One day a young woman came to the temple to receive her own endowment. Prior to giving her instructions, I just said to her: "Well, how are you today?"

She answered, "Oh, I am so nervous!"

I said, "Tell me why you are nervous."

She paused, and then with deep feeling she said, "Because, think about it—I am in Heavenly Father's house." The tears began to flow as she added: "I am a convert to the Church, and from the day I joined this Church I have lived for this moment. Now it is finally here, and I am so overwhelmed that I can hardly absorb it."

If only we could each feel that kind of humility and exhilaration each time we entered the Lord's house!

∞

President Heber J. Grant observed: "Do the Latter-day Saints who have the privilege of entering our holy temples, appreciate the great blessing that is given to them, and do they, in very deed, realize . . . that they are treading upon 'holy ground'?" (*Gospel Standards,* 276).

There is inscribed on every temple this statement: *Holiness to the Lord, The House of the Lord.* President Gordon B. Hinckley has said that it might say, *Holiness is the House of the Lord.* That means exactly what it says. When we go to the temple, we enter God's house here on earth. What a remarkable gift to have such a place!

THE TEMPLE IS THE KEY TO OUR HAPPINESS

That great Kirtland Temple dedicatory prayer concludes with this emotional plea: "And let these, thine anointed ones, be clothed with salvation, and thy saints shout aloud for joy. Amen, and Amen" (D&C 109:80). The Prophet

Joseph understood that we could never know complete joy and happiness without the blessings of the temple.

In the Book of Mormon, King Benjamin taught us of the great plan of happiness brought about by the redemption of our Savior. When King Benjamin called all his people to the temple just prior to his death, he counseled them: "And moreover, I would desire that ye should consider on the blessed and happy state of those that keep the commandments of God. For behold, they are blessed in all things, both temporal and spiritual; and if they hold out faithful to the end they are received into heaven, that thereby they may dwell with God in a state of never-ending happiness. O remember, remember that these things are true; for the Lord God hath spoken it" (Mosiah 2:41).

We want to be happy. God wants us to be happy. It is a gift that God offers freely to those who satisfy the preconditions. We want to be with our families eternally and live in the presence of God. Those blessings are promised to those who seek to understand and apply the eternal truths the Lord makes available to each of us in His holy temples.

The temple is the key to finding happiness, both in this life and in eternity. It is the Lord's spiritual university on earth, and our understanding of its profound symbolic teachings can be unlocked only through a course of worthiness, preparation, searching, pondering, and asking the questions that will open our minds and hearts to the things of God. In the temple the Lord defines the pathway to the great plan of happiness.

⌒

Kathleen: When I was growing up my parents would often recount stories of our pioneer ancestry. Their great love and deep appreciation for the sacrifices of those wonderful people was shared on many occasions. I came to know my forefathers long before I understood how important it is to feel a connection to those who have gone before. Today there hangs on my wall a framed group of pictures showing eight generations of women who form my matriarchal line. There are times when I look at them and remember that someday I will account to them for my life's journey. When that day comes, I want to embrace them and thank them for their faithfulness to the Lord, which has formed the foundation of my life. My heart has truly been turned to the hearts of my ancestors, and I am now trying to pass along to my posterity the promises made to each of us if we are faithful.

Richard: Because my father died when I was an infant, I have never known any association with him in mortality. I have yearned to know him, and as I grew I would ask friends and family members what he was like. I had an insatiable desire to know his personality and his personal traits. It was my mother who helped me come to know him. She would often tell me of his goodness and his love of the Lord. She would tell me how very much he loved me and how thankful he was that I had been sent to their home. I have often wondered what it will be like on that day when we finally meet and embrace each other. Because of the great love and teachings of my mother, my heart has truly been turned to my father, and his to me. I have felt his powerful influence for good in my life. My obligation now is to live and serve in such a way that when I am reunited with him, I will feel that I have done all in my power to honor his name and that of my dear mother.

∞

Each of us has become aware that the principle of eternal happiness would not be complete without the results of the sacred sealing powers that bind our families together eternally. Our service in the Salt Lake Temple has embedded in our hearts a deep and abiding love for His holy house. We keenly recognize that for those who will prepare their hearts and lives and commit themselves to search and learn in the temple, there will begin to flow into their lives a river of "living water." The Savior promised to the young woman who sought water at the well: "But whosoever drinketh of the water that I shall give him shall never thirst; but the water that I shall give him shall be in him a well of water springing up into everlasting life" (John 4:14).

It is recorded in chapters 40 through 46 of the book of Ezekiel that a heavenly ministrant showed Ezekiel in vision the temple to be built in Jerusalem. After showing him the details of the building of the temple, he then taught Ezekiel the importance of the temple: "Afterward he brought me again unto the door of the house; and, behold, waters issued out from under the threshold of the house . . . and it was a river. . . . And it shall come to pass, that every thing that liveth, . . . whithersoever the rivers shall come, shall live . . . for they shall be healed" (Ezekiel 47:1, 5, 9).

The house of the Lord becomes as a "river of life" for each of us. As we drink from its waters, it not only heals us but also links our families together and provides the plan whereby eternal happiness may become a reality.

The importance of those family bonds is made clear by the words of the angel Moroni to the Prophet Joseph Smith on September 21, 1823: "Behold, I will reveal unto you the Priesthood, by the hand of Elijah the prophet, before the

*May we each recognize that our Heavenly
Father's plan of eternal happiness finds fulfillment
only through the blessings and covenants made
available to us in the house of the Lord.*

coming of the great and dreadful day of the Lord. And he shall plant in the hearts of the children the promises made to the fathers, and the hearts of the children shall turn to their fathers. *If it were not so, the whole earth would be utterly wasted at his coming*" (D&C 2:1–3; emphasis added).

Think of the implications of that statement. The Lord will plant in the hearts of the children the promises made to the fathers (that is, the promises made in the temple), and the hearts of the children will turn to their fathers. Therein is the great key. Therein is the mission of the Savior fulfilled regarding the "immortality and eternal life of man" (Moses 1:39). Only in the temples of the Lord can the great welding link of families be completed.

In other words, if this great work of the temples were not accomplished, then the entire purpose of the creation of the earth would be nullified.

Christians the world over are familiar with the story of the creation of the earth. To most it is a story of organizing matter into a world and filling it with living things. But few understand the overriding purpose of that creation. It is far more than just a pretty story. It is the foundation from which all other portions of our Father's plan evolve.

May we each recognize that our Heavenly Father's plan of eternal happiness finds fulfillment only through the blessings and covenants made available to us in the house of the Lord. It is there, in the temple, that the "living waters" promised by the Savior await us. May we have the wisdom to understand the importance of what is offered to each of us. May we prepare our lives. May we go to the temple. May we search and learn. May the plan of happiness be a reality in our lives.

May the temple truly become a house of learning and a great source of revelation and blessing in our lives.

SOURCES

Bednar, David A. "Seek Learning by Faith." *Ensign,* September 2007, 60–68.

Christofferson, D. Todd. "A Sense of the Sacred." *Liahona,* June 2006, 28–31.

"The Family: A Proclamation to the World." *Ensign,* November 1995, 102.

Grant, Heber J. *Gospel Standards: Selections from the Sermons and Writings of Heber J. Grant.* Compiled by G. Homer Durham. Salt Lake City: Deseret Book, 1981

Lund, Gerald N. "Opening Our Hearts." *Ensign,* May 2008, 32–34.

Merriam-Webster's Collegiate Dictionary, 11th ed. Springfield, Massachusetts: Merriam-Webster, Inc., 2003.

Nelson, Russell M. "Faith in Jesus Christ." *Ensign,* March 2008, 24–30.

Oaks, Dallin H. "Powerful Ideas." *Ensign,* November 1995, 25–27.

Packer, Boyd K. *The Holy Temple.* Salt Lake City: Bookcraft, 1980.

————. "Personal Revelation: The Gift, the Test, and the Promise," *Ensign,* November 1994, 59–61.

————. "Reverence Invites Revelation." *Ensign,* November 1991, 21–23.

"Recollections of the Prophet Joseph Smith." *Juvenile Instructor,* vol. 27 (July 1, 1892).

Richards, Franklin D. "A Tour of Historic Scenes." *Contributor,* May 1886, 301.

Romney, Marion G. "Reverence." *Ensign,* September 1982, 2–5.

Widtsoe, John A. "Temple Worship." *Utah Genealogical and Historical Magazine,* April 1921, 49–64.

INDEX